● Changing the Guard

The monarch has been guarded since Tudor times and today's colourful and popular Changing the Guard – or Guard Mounting – is a ceremonial occasion which happens daily in the summer at Buckingham Palace. The Foot Guards comprises soldiers from the Grenadier Guards, the Coldstream Guards, the Scots Guards, the Irish Guards and the Welsh Guards regiments. They are recognized by their scarlet uniforms

and bearskin caps. The ceremony itself lasts for about half an hour. The Guard is changed, watched by admiring onlookers, in a dazzling display of pageantry and military precision. *www. changing-the-guard.com*

● Royal Mews

This is where the Queen's horses are stabled, and royal carriages and motor cars used in ceremonies and processions are also kept here. The old Royal Mews, at Charing Cross, was where the royal hawks were kept at moulting or 'mew' time, hence the name. The present Mews, built by John Nash in 1825 in the grounds of Buckingham Palace, houses 30 horses (Cleveland Bays and Windsor Greys) in gleaming stables, and the magnificent coaches used on ceremonial occasions, including the Gold State Coach. The Royal Mews is open during the early spring, summer and early autumn. *www.royalcollection.org.uk*

ROYAL CONNECTIONS

● Banqueting House

Historic Royal Palaces look after this unique building on Whitehall which is all that remains of the original Palace of Whitehall, destroyed by fire in 1698. Inigo Jones' Banqueting House is classical Italian Renaissance, and was the first English building in this style. It is built on three floors with a double-height banqueting hall that has a gorgeous ceiling painted by Sir Peter Paul Rubens. *www.hrp.org.uk*

● Horse Guards

Horse Guards on Whitehall is built on the yard where Henry VIII used to joust. Now a low archway is guarded by two mounted troopers of the Household Cavalry. The archway leads to Horse Guards Parade, where Her Majesty the Queen takes the salute at Trooping the Colour each year. Changing the Guard is at 11am Monday–Saturday (10am on Sunday).

● Kensington Palace

Members of the British Royal Family live in this 17th-century palace, built when Kensington was a village. Christopher Wren redesigned the original building and now the Duke and Duchess of Gloucester, the Duke and Duchess of Kent, and Prince and Princess Michael of Kent all have apartments here. Kensington Palace was home to the late Diana, Princess of Wales, whose sons Princes William and Harry were brought up here. Princess Margaret lived in this palace until her death in 2002. The state rooms are open to the public and managed by Historic Royal Palaces. *www.hrp.org.uk*

● The Royal Parks

Everyone can enjoy 2,000 hectares (5,000 acres) of beautiful parkland, once the private preserve of the Royal Family, in the heart of the city. The eight parks are Bushy Park, Greenwich Park, Hyde Park, Kensington Gardens, Richmond Park, St James's Park, The Green Park and The Regent's Park. Hyde Park and Kensington Gardens, linked by The Serpentine lake, make the largest open space in central London. Each park is carefully looked after with renowned gardens, trees, entertainment and historic buildings. *www.royalparks.org.uk*

HISTORIC BUILDINGS

● Houses of Parliament

The 98-m (320-ft) clock tower that holds Big Ben, the bell with the famous chimes, towers above the Palace of Westminster which contains the House of Commons, the House of Lords and Westminster Hall. This has been the seat of British government since the 13th century, and is where the country's laws are debated and put in place. The statue outside is of Oliver Cromwell who, in the 17th century, ensured the supremacy of parliament over the monarchy. The Houses of Parliament are open for pre-booked tours and visits. *www.parliament.uk*

● Tower of London

At the heart of this impressive complex of buildings on the bank of the Thames is the White Tower, four-square and solid, built by William the Conqueror in 1078 as a fortress for the new Norman rule. Over the centuries other towers and buildings have been constructed within concentric walls and a moat. The Tower, which has been the home of the Crown Jewels of the United Kingdom since 1303, has served as royal palace and prison, place of torture and execution, armoury and Royal Mint, a zoo and, briefly, an observatory. Visitors are looked after by the Yeomen Warders or 'Beefeaters', who wear a distinctive red uniform that dates from Tudor times. Legend has it that should the ravens – who have inhabited the Tower for centuries – leave, the monarchy and kingdom will fall. *www.hrp.org.uk/TowerOfLondon/*

● Tower Bridge

A new crossing of the River Thames downstream from London Bridge was urgently needed in the late 19th century – but it had to be one that allowed shipping to pass safely into the Pool of London. So Sir John Wolfe Barry came up with a design for two towers, linked by a bascule bridge – one with 'arms' or

'bascules' that move by means of a counterweight. Tower Bridge, opened in 1894, is recognized the world over as a symbol of London. Visitors may enjoy the views from the high walkways linking the towers and admire the magnificent Victorian engineering room. *www.towerbridge.org.uk*

● Shakespeare's Globe

In 1599, when William Shakespeare belonged to acting company The Lord Chamberlain's Men, the Globe Theatre was built alongside the Thames at Southwark. Just 13 years later it burnt down when a cannon misfired during a performance of *Henry VIII*. The Globe was soon rebuilt, but eventually closed in the Puritan backlash of the early 1640s. American director Sam Wanamaker founded the Shakespeare Globe Trust which has faithfully recreated the Globe not far from the original site. It opened in 1997. You can see plays and take tours from May to October, and enjoy tours, occasional theatre and exhibitions in the winter months. *www.shakespearesglobe.org*

● Apsley House

'Number One, London', as this grand 18th-century mansion is often called, stands in splendid isolation at Hyde Park Corner. Designed by Robert Adam for Lord Apsley, then Lord Chancellor, the house was eventually bought by the Duke of Wellington. It is his fabulous art collection that can be seen here, including Canova's magnificent sculpture of Napoleon that dominates the entrance hall. The house is now run by English Heritage. *www.english-heritage.org.uk*

● Somerset House

This great building in the Strand was home to many public offices, including the Registrar General and the Admiralty. But in the late-20th century the building became a centre for the visual arts, including the Courtauld Gallery (see page 28), and the terrace overlooking the Thames was opened as a summer café-bar. Now there is a programme of concerts, films, workshops, and art and design exhibitions. The visitor centre tells the story of this neo-classical building which still houses the gilded state barge of the Lord Mayor of the City of London. *www.somersethouse.org.uk*

STREET SCENES

London Eye & the South Bank

One of the world's tallest observation wheels is the major attraction on London's South Bank – the riverside that runs along the Thames between Lambeth and Blackfriars Bridges. But here you will also find the Royal Festival Hall, the city's main concert hall, Queen Elizabeth Hall, the Hayward Gallery and the National Theatre. Nearby are the Old Vic and the Young Vic theatres and two film theatres, including the BFI Imax cinema which shows larger-than-life images, sometimes in 3D. The London Aquarium is found in the old County Hall, while there are riverside walks and pleasant quaysides where you can eat and drink and watch the world walk by. The *Golden Hinde*, a replica of Francis Drake's ship, is a short walk along the river. *www.southbanklondon.com*

Piccadilly Circus

Here, where the bright lights of theatreland beckon and traffic whizzes round the statue popularly known as Eros, the God of Love, five streets converge and tourists meet to shop in Regents Street and Piccadilly (named after a 'piccadill', a frilled collar made here 300 years ago). The statue of a naked winged archer, cast in aluminium and set above a dramatic fountain, is a memorial to Victorian politician and philanthropist Lord Shaftesbury. The statue, by sculptor Alfred Gilbert, is sometimes called The Angel of Christian Charity and, more popularly, Eros – but it was always intended to be his brother Anteros, an altogether more sober character.

Downing Street

There are security gates now at the entrance to Downing Street where Britain's Prime Minister and Chancellor of the Exchequer have their official homes and where the office of the government's Chief Whip is situated. But there is still – officially – a public right of way down this street past one of the world's most famous addresses, Number 10, where the Prime Minister lives. The Chancellor lives next door, at number 11. Downing Street is off Whitehall, just a few minutes' walk from the Palace of Westminster, where the British Parliament sits, and a little further from Buckingham Palace.

Trafalgar Square

This enormous square, dominated by Nelson's Column, commemorates the Battle of Trafalgar (1805), a British victory in the Napoleonic Wars. At the base of the column are impressive fountains, designed by Sir Edwin Lutyens, and four enormous bronze lions by Sir Edwin Landseer. Trafalgar Square is where people congregate to celebrate the New Year, for great national events and to make political protest. www.london.gov.uk/trafalgarsquare

Notting Hill

This cosmopolitan area of London to the north of Kensington is a large, fashionable, affluent area with attractive houses, high-class shopping and restaurants alongside more modest streets. Notting Hill became well-known when a film of the same name became a hit in 1999. Since 1964 the colourful Notting Hill Carnival has been celebrated here every year in late August.

MARKETS

● Covent Garden

In the Middle Ages there was indeed a garden here – a convent garden, supplying St Peter's Abbey with fresh fruit and vegetables. In the early-17th century Inigo Jones designed a great square here with a market at its centre. Covent Garden became a place of street entertainment, market trading and prostitution. From the 18th century a great wholesale fruit, flower and vegetable market flourished until 1974, when it was relocated and the present fashionable mix of shops, craft markets, bars and cafés, street performances and entertainment became established. The Royal Opera House and the church of St Paul's both face on to the market. *www.coventgardenlondonuk.com*

● Camden Market

Hundreds of thousands of people visit this group of markets near Camden Lock on the Regents Canal each week. Five separate markets operate, selling everything from designer goods to antiques, from shoes to food. The main selling days are Saturdays and Sundays, but increasingly more business is done on weekdays. *www.camdenmarkets.org*

● Brick Lane Market

Every Sunday morning the northern end of Brick Lane, in Tower Hamlets, is full of market stalls selling a variety of objects from antiques to bicycles. It's a favourite with photographers and bargain-hunters alike.

● Portobello Road Market

Famous for its second-hand clothes and antiques, this street market in Portobello Road, Notting Hill, is one of London's best. Throughout the week you can buy fruit and vegetables here but the main day for antiques is Saturday when tourists and locals alike look for bargains.

● Borough Market

This flourishing market – a mix of wholesale and retail – has become a fashionable place to buy food and flowers, with a reputation for selling fine foods from around the world. London's oldest food market (it claims to have been established in Roman times) has occupied its present site for a quarter of a century. It has an art deco entrance from Southwark Street and has featured in films, including *Bridget Jones's Diary* and *Harry Potter and the Prisoner of Azkaban.*
www.boroughmarket.org.uk

POPULAR ATTRACTIONS

● Madame Tussauds

The young Frenchwoman Anna-Maria Grosholtz learnt how to make wax models under the tutelage of Dr Philippe Curtis. She made death masks during the French Revolution and, married to Francois Tussaud, came to London in 1802 with her unique collection of waxworks. She opened her famous museum as The Baker Street Bazaar in 1835, charging sixpence (2½p) to see the likenesses. The name has changed and the collection grown to include the Royal Family, film stars and celebrities. Now in Marylebone Road, the Chamber of Horrors still thrills, as does the Spirit of London, a 'taxi ride' through a model of London. You can also get a glimpse of the art of waxwork-making. *www.madametussauds.com*

● Harrods

One of the world's largest and most famous department stores started as a small wholesale grocer's shop in 1834 in London's East End. Charles Henry Harrod moved his business to Knightsbridge, opening a retail store with three staff in 1849. His son, also Charles, worked to expand the business which by 1880 had diversified and now employed 100 people. Two years later a fire destroyed the whole operation. But this enabled rebuilding on a grander scale. Towards the end of the century a 'moving staircase' was installed – nervous customers were offered a tot of brandy to revive them after using it. Today Harrods offers a huge variety of goods in more than 330 departments. *www.harrods.com*

● Lord's Cricket Ground

In St John's Wood you'll find not only the home of cricket but also the world's oldest sporting museum. Owned by the MCC (Marylebone Cricket Club) the present Lord's is the third, founded by Thomas Lord in the 19th century. It was opened in 1814 with a match between the MCC and Hertfordshire. More than one hundred test matches have been played at the ground that is a place of pilgrimage to many cricket fans. The MCC Museum has been collecting some of the most important cricket memorabilia in the world since 1864. *www.lords.org*

● London Zoo

More than 16,000 animals from 755 species, many of them endangered and uncommon, like the Tasmanian devil and the long-nosed potaroo, live in the 14 hectares (36 acres) of Regent's Park that is ZSL London Zoo. The zoo, established for scientific purposes in 1828, was opened to the public 20 years later. It is the world's oldest scientific zoo and also the first to establish an aquarium, reptile and insect houses, and a children's zoo (now renamed 'Animal Adventure'). The larger species, such as elephants and rhinos, are at ZSL Whipsnade in Bedfordshire. *www.zsl.org*

● The London Dungeon

Here you'll experience at close hand some of the gruesome practices of the past when medieval prisoners were tortured to make them talk. Events and people in London's history, such as the Great Fire of 1666, the Plague, Sweeney Todd and Jack the Ripper, are brought to life with actors, while braver visitors can participate in a variety of ways. The dungeon is set in dark vaults beneath London Bridge station. *www.thedungeons.com*

● Westminster Abbey

This great Gothic building near the Palace of Westminster has seen the coronation of most British monarchs over the past 900 years, and the burial of many in the Abbey's St Edward the Confessor's Chapel. Parts of the building are 11th century but the 13th and 14th centuries were when most of what you see today was built. Here you'll find the Grave of the Unknown Warrior, a moving tribute to the unidentified soldiers who died in the First World War, and also Poets' Corner where many great British poets, including Blake, Shelley, Burns, Tennyson, Wordsworth and Byron, are remembered. The Abbey, whose official name is The Collegiate Church of St Peter at Westminster, was briefly a cathedral in the mid-16th century and is a royal peculiar – falling directly under the jurisdiction of the monarch rather than a diocese.
www.westminster-abbey.org

Architect Sir Christopher Wren was already drawing up designs for a new cathedral to replace the existing St Paul's on Ludgate Hill before the Great Fire of 1666 destroyed the old cathedral. Work on the great structure began in 1677 and the building, crowned with its enormous dome, was completed on Wren's 76th birthday in 1708. St Paul's, built on the City of London's highest point, is the seat of the Bishop of London and contains hundreds of memorials to significant British figures. It has played host to many great occasions including the funeral of Winston Churchill and the wedding of Prince Charles and Princess Diana. *www.stpauls.co.uk*

CATHEDRALS & CHURCHES

● The Temple Church

Tucked away between Fleet Street and the River Thames is a quiet oasis of ancient buildings, including the beautiful and historic Temple Church, consecrated in 1185 for the Knights Templar, the Christian soldiers of the Middle Ages. The church is constructed in two parts – the Round Church, which echoes the circular Church of the Holy Sepulchre in Jerusalem, and the Chancel. Now the church is used by members of two Inns of Court, the Middle and Inner Temples. It is well known for the excellence of its music – and for the fact that it figures prominently in the popular novel and film *The Da Vinci Code*. www.templechurch.com

● Westminster Cathedral

Walk into the piazza in front of this, the country's leading Roman Catholic church, in Victoria, and you'll find an extraordinary façade that owes much to the early Christian Byzantine movement. Designed by John Bentley, towers, domes and balconies decorate the front of this red brick and white Portland stone building, where worship started in 1903. Inside, much of the decoration, including mosaics, sculpture, kneelers and inlaid ebony, was made by members of the Arts and Crafts movement. The 14 stations of the cross were carved out of limestone by sculptor Eric Gill.
www.westminstercathedral.org.uk

● St Martin-in-the-Fields

The 'church with the ever-open door' in a corner of Trafalgar Square is famous for its work with homeless people, its concerts at lunchtimes and evenings, and its café in the crypt. It's the parish church of the Royal Family, with whom it has close connections, and notables such as furniture-maker Thomas Chippendale are buried here. The present rectangular building with its high steeple was designed by James Gibbs in 1721. *www.stmartin-in-the-fields.org*

19

MUSEUMS

● British Museum

This is one of the world's great museums, representing culture drawn from across nations. The museum, in Bloomsbury, with its colonnaded portico and its inner court designed by Sir Norman Foster, is among London's top attractions, with around seven million objects in the collections.

They include the sculptures of the Parthenon Frieze, the Rosetta Stone, which allowed Egyptologists to decipher hieroglyphics, and the Portland Vase, a violet-blue Roman cameo vase. The British Library was once part of the museum but is now housed in Euston Road, near St Pancras Station. *www.britishmuseum.org*

● Natural History Museum

The soaring exhibition halls of this South Kensington museum are a favourite with children clamouring to see the famous dinosaur skeletons and reconstructions. Once part of the British Museum, the collections were transferred to this airy building in 1881. An incredible 70 million exhibits cover five main collections: plants, insects, prehistoric creatures, minerals and zoology. The most popular exhibits include the skeleton of Dippy the dinosaur (*Diplodocus carnegeii*) and the skeleton of a blue whale, lying alongside a model of the same huge creature. *www.nhm.ac.uk*

Victoria & Albert Museum

The world's largest and greatest museum of art and design became the V&A in 1899, although it had started life in 1852. The huge museum in Cromwell Gardens, South Kensington, houses nearly five million objects, some of them 3,000 years old. There are collections of decorative and artistic material including ceramics, glass, prints, textiles, silver, costume, fashion and jewellery, sculpture, Asian and Islamic art. Children love the gruesome Tippoo's Tiger – a life-size mechanical tiger devouring a European soldier. *www.vam.ac.uk*

Science Museum

This is the third of the trio of world-famous museums (the others are the V&A and the Natural History Museum) established in Victorian times in South Kensington. Here you can explore space and see the earliest steam engines, including Stephenson's *Rocket* and *Puffing Billy*, or the first jet engine. You can learn about the structure of DNA and explore medical history or see the evidence for climate change. There are hundreds of interactive exhibits designed to bring science alive. *www.sciencemuseum.org.uk*

Churchill War Rooms

The command centre for the British Government during the Second World War was an underground set of rooms beneath Whitehall. Here the cabinet met regularly and a suite was provided for Winston Churchill, his family and close advisers. Now the War Rooms are open to the public and part of the space, including Churchill's private rooms, has been turned into a museum celebrating the wartime leader's life. The whole complex is a branch of the Imperial War Museum. *www.iwm.org.uk*

MUSEUMS

HMS *Belfast*

A campaign to save this Royal Navy town-class cruiser successfully saw her restored and put into service as a museum ship, moored near Tower Bridge in the Pool of London. Damaged badly by a mine in the Second World War, *Belfast* (launched in the city of the same name in 1938 at the Harland and Wolff shipyard) went on to escort Arctic convoys, and take part in the Battle of North Cape and the D-Day landings. She is now a branch of the Imperial War Museum. *www.iwm.org.uk/belfast*

Household Cavalry Museum

In this historic building you will find troopers working with the horses that are stabled here. The Household Cavalry Museum, inside Horse Guards (see page 4), contains a unique collection of antique uniforms, silverware, gallantry awards, musical instruments and even a cork leg which once belonged to the Earl of Uxbridge. The Household Cavalry consists of two senior regiments – the Life Guards and the Blues and Royals. It serves to guard members of the Royal Family and sees active duty around the world. *www.householdcavalrymuseum.co.uk*

Guards Museum

The five regiments of Foot Guards whose story this museum tells are the Grenadier Guards, Coldstream Guards, Welsh Guards, Scots Guards and Irish Guards. With the two regiments of the Household Cavalry, they make up Her Majesty's Household Division and guard the monarch and the royal palaces. This museum, at Wellington Barracks, Birdcage Walk, contains artefacts, documents and information about the regiments. *www.theguardsmuseum.com*

Museum of London

Here is the story of London told through a series of galleries, taking you from prehistoric days, through Roman times to the Saxons and Middle Ages, Tudors and Stuarts, to explore the growth of a great city. New galleries take as their starting point the Great Fire of 1666 after which much of the old city was rebuilt. The museum, at London Wall, is largely concerned with the social history of London and its people. *www.museumoflondon.org.uk*

Museum of London Docklands

In this former sugar warehouse on West India Quay in Canary Wharf you'll find the history of London as one of the world's leading ports, through tales of trade, migration and commerce. It's a long and interesting story, starting with the Romans, who built a city here

and revealing how the docklands were regenerated in the late-20th century. *www.museumindocklands.org.uk*

MUSEUMS

● National Maritime Museum

The largest maritime museum in England and possibly the world, this museum, which incorporates the Royal Observatory with its Astronomy Centre and Planetarium, and the historic Queen's House, has more than two million exhibits, including maps, maritime art, models, manuscripts and navigational instruments. Set in the magnificent 80-hectare (200-acre) Greenwich Royal Park, the Maritime Museum reflects the great seafaring history and tradition of the British Isles. *www.nmm.ac.uk*

● Royal Observatory

Here is the famous Longitude 0° line where you can stand with one leg in the western hemisphere and one in the eastern, simply by straddling the Prime Meridian – the centre of world time and space. In October 1884 the International Meridian Conference voted that the Prime Meridian should be internationally recognized as Longitude 0°. The Observatory, which incorporates an Astronomy Centre, was set up by Charles II in the 17th century specifically to discover how to measure longitude and improve navigation. He created the position of Astronomer Royal to serve as director of the observatory. *www.rog.nmm.ac.uk*

Imperial War Museum

The five national branches of this museum exist to allow people to understand modern war and the impact it has on society. The London museum, at Southwark, houses important collections of official and personal documents, photographs, film, and video and oral history recordings. There is art from war fronts, military hardware and equipment to be seen here. *www.iwm.org.uk*

London Transport Museum

The red double-decker bus is regarded the world over as a symbol of London. But a visit to the London Transport Museum, located in a Victorian steel and glass building at Covent Garden, shows a huge range of vehicles. There are trams and trolleybuses, buses, taxis and rail vehicles, including a steam locomotive from the old Metropolitan Railway, the world's first underground system that eventually became the London Underground. *www.ltmuseum.co.uk*

Benjamin Franklin House

Scientist, diplomat, inventor, founding father of the United States of America, Benjamin Franklin lodged at 36 Craven Street between 1757 and 1775. Now the house has become a museum showing Franklin's life in London and in its wider context. Dramatic performance brings to life the conflict, political tension and triumph, and daily living while visitors explore the listed Georgian house. *www.benjaminfranklinhouse.org*

ART GALLERIES

● Tate Modern

Climb to the top of this converted power station on the Southbank, now London's most popular art gallery, where you can eat in the restaurant with long views over the city. Tate Modern, one of the two Tate galleries in London, houses international contemporary and modern art from 1900, including works by Henry Moore, Matisse, Dali, Picasso, Anish Kapoor and Mark Rothko. Two floors show off the permanent collections while the enormous Turbine Hall houses large specially-commissioned modern work. Another floor is big enough for two temporary exhibitions of large work. *www.tate.org.uk*

● Tate Britain

Here you will find work by British artists of the past 600 years. The Tate opened in Millbank in 1897 as The National Gallery of British Art but was soon known by the name of its founder, the sugar magnate Sir Henry Tate. It became Tate Britain when Tate Modern was opened in March 2000. The most comprehensive collection of paintings by J.M.W. Turner is held here in the Clore Gallery which was designed by architect James Stirling. The work of 20th and 21st century artists on display includes David Hockney, Peter Blake, Francis Bacon, Tracey Emin, Damien Hirst and Sam Taylor-Wood. The often controversial Turner Prize entries are exhibited here. *www.tate.org.uk*

National Gallery

Only the façade of the National Gallery, facing Trafalgar Square, has remained unchanged since its completion in 1838. It was founded earlier, in 1824 in Pall Mall, with the acquisition of just 38 pieces, including paintings by Raphael and Hogarth. The Trafalgar Square building allowed expansion and now houses one of the great collections of the world with over 2,300 works from the mid-13th century to 1900, representing most major movements in Western European art. During the Second World War the paintings were removed to various locations in Wales for safety.

www.nationalgallery.org.uk

National Portrait Gallery

This is a gallery where the paintings are chosen for the significance of the subject, rather than that of the artist. The portraits of thousands of famous Britons are housed here. When the National Portrait Gallery opened in 1856 it was the first of its kind in the world. Its first exhibit was the world-famous so-called 'Chandos' painting said to be of William Shakespeare. The gallery moved to St Martin's Place in 1896. Here you can see paintings ranging from portraits of the British Royal Family to Branwell Bronte's depiction of his three famous sisters. *www.npg.org.uk*

ART GALLERIES

● Royal Academy

The Royal Academy of Arts is an independent body, run by artists and architects with the aim of encouraging people to talk about and understand art and design. Founded by George III in 1768, it achieves its aim through exhibitions, debate and education. The annual Summer Show at the Academy in Burlington House, Piccadilly, is open for all to enter and works are chosen on merit. The Royal Academy is run by 80 elected Academicians, all of whom are artists or architects.
www.royalacademy.org.uk

● Courtauld Gallery

This is the gallery belonging to the Courtauld Institute of Art, one of the world's leading art history centres. The gallery was begun by Samuel Courtauld in 1932 with a gift of outstanding French Impressionist and Post-Impressionist paintings. It holds many important collections housed in the Strand Building of Somerset House, which was the first home of the Royal Academy (see above) on its foundation in 1768.
www.courtauld.ac.uk

● Wallace Collection

Here is an unrivalled collection of superb Old Master paintings, furniture, ceramics, arms and armour, sculpture, glass and enamel, gold boxes and miniatures, arranged in 25 galleries. The museum, opened to the public in 1900 in Hertford House, Manchester Square, and still there today, was left to the nation by the widow of art collector Sir Richard Wallace. A condition was that no piece should ever leave the collection, even on loan. *www.wallacecollection.org*